FULL THROTTLE

HIGH OCTANE INSIGHTS ON ACHIEVING YOUR DREAMS

CARL CREASMAN

Full Throttle

High Octane Insights On Achieving Your Dreams

This PDF is special.

It contains features similar to a web page along with links to pages on the Internet.

Use your keyboard arrows or page up/down buttons to navigate from page to page. Try the full screen mode button at the bottom of this page to hide background clutter. The ESCAPE key returns you to regular viewing.

NOTE: Some features only work in the FREE ADOBE ACROBAT READER. If you use other PDF readers such as the Mac PREVIEW, feature such as Full Screen and soft page turns won't work.

Click here to zoom to a full screen view. Click again to exit full screen view.

Navigate to the previous page

Navigate to the next page

©2010 Carl Creasman

Full Throttle

High Octane Insights On Achieving Your Dreams

Copyright © 2010, Carl E. Creasman, Jr.

All rights reserved.
No part of this book may be used or reproduced in any manner whatsoever without the written permission of the author and the publisher, except for brief excerpts quoted in critical reviews.

Published by:
Carl E. Creasman, Jr.
P.O. Box 217
Winter Park, FL 32790

www.carlcreasman.com

Printed in the United States of America
Interactive Ebook design by
www.TheBookProducer.com

ISBN #: 978-0-9814638-1-0

Contents

©2010 Carl Creasman

Introduction

Once upon a time, I wanted to buy a motorcycle. No, scratch that, once upon a time, I wanted to be cool. Uh, well, maybe, once upon a time I wanted other people to think I was cool, so I wanted a motorcycle. Probably a little bit of both—I thought it would make me cool, and I thought others would think I was cool. Unfortunately, getting a bike when it would have mattered, back in high school, wasn't going to happen. This story, then, is about my decision to pursue this 30-year-old dream from my youth and the lessons that emerged from the journey.

Now realize that my story is a pretty simple one. I wanted to get a motorcycle; easy enough. Yet, through the process, I saw my experience as a clear example of what I teach to others about "living their dreams," accomplishing the things you wish for your life. Many people that I mentor wish to pursue a dream, wish for a successful life, yet never really seem to know how to get there.

I wrote *Success for Life: Answers to the 77 Questions College Students Ask* with the hopes that some of my

answers would provide a simple roadmap to success. Those who have read it have seen that truth in my words, but some still struggle to move from theory into practice. That's where this book comes in. As I went through the process, I knew that a series of critical lessons had happened to me, either in the "getting the bike" phase or in my experiences riding in the first years of ownership.

One key point to make at the outset is that you should not dismiss your dreams that are "small" or "normal." So often when speakers or mentors talk about "dreams" or "life goals" it sounds so massive that it paralyzes. And yes, many that I mentor have dreams that are huge. There's nothing wrong with that, but at the same time, it is okay to accomplish dreams that are simpler. Maybe your dream is to take 6 months to tour the country in an RV. Maybe your dream is to start your own rock band or write a book of poetry. Maybe your dream is, like the movie *Julie and Julia,* to spend a year engaging in a passion or hobby.

Sure, we need "life goals" that can help guide us on the overall journey. I want you to find *Success for Life,*

©2010 Carl Creasman

but that concept of success for life does not have to mean only one overriding dream and you either succeed or fail. On the contrary, it means a life lived well; always being a person of excellence who considers the world around them and dreams for better.

Through the process of deciding to get a motorcycle and then through the first months on my bike, I realized that the journey highlighted concrete examples of various aspects of living a successful life. You have to have a dream. You must decide on goals to accomplish that dream. You need to know yourself, your limits and your handicaps. You need to be prepared for a possible negative outcome and you need to take responsibility for what happens next.

We will explore these and other concepts in the pages that follow. So, come on and join me on the open road as we ride through life.

Follow your dreams: Riding like The "Fonz"

In 1974, when I was 10 years old, a TV show aired called *Happy Days.* This show was an idealized reflection of life in the 1950s and stared Ron Howard as Ritchie Cunningham. For my family, this show became a staple in our house, especially as my sister and I made the transition to high school. Each Tuesday we would watch Richie and his friends, Potsie and Ralph Malph, navigate their way through situations and issues, some quite serious like racism or nuclear warfare and others merely silly high school things like dating or your first kiss.

However, if you remember the series at all, you know that the real "leading" character was one that surprised the shows' creators. Arthur Fonzarelli, the "Fonz" initially was a "side character," a high school dropout who was just casually Richie's friend. He played something of a sweetheart tough guy, a ladies man who could be called on

©2010 Carl Creasman

to help get Richie out of some tough jams with other local "toughs." Yet, by the third year of the series, the popularity of "Fonzie" with the fans raised his profile and helped the actor, Henry Winkler, move to some degree of fame and stardom.

The connection with Fonzie was, in part, something to do with the Sixties; young people like myself, coming of age in the 1970s, subconsciously knew we had "missed it." Fonzie was a rebel in the TV show and so by connecting to him, we were able to loosely express the same sense of rebellion as teens of 8-10 years before had.

The other connection with Fonzie was his motorcycle. *Easy Rider*, the powerful movie about the Sixties had come out in 1969 and clearly positioned the motorcycle as a vehicle with an attitude, the rebellious ride. The motorcycle gang, Hells Angels, had been around since post-world war 2, growing in notoriety through the '50s and then gaining some infamous attention with their knife-wielding episode at the music festival in Altamonte, CA supposedly protecting the band "The Rolling Stones". Tie those references with other famous scenes such as the movie *The Wild Ones*

)10 Carl Creasman www.CarlCreasman.com

or *The Great Escape* with Steve McQueen's famous riding scene and the motorcycle was connected to freedom, power and rebellion. Fonzie rode into our family rooms with that same motif.

As a kid in the countryside of East Tennessee, most of my friends began getting motorcycles at the age of 9 or 10, at the same time as *Happy Days* started—1974. I wanted to join my "wild" friends racing through the country on a "dirt bike." My parents had a different opinion.

For my Mom, the point was safety. If there has ever been a mother who personified the concept of the "overprotective mother," it was my mom. I love my mother to death, but she has always been a bit on the scared side, particularly as it relates to my sister and I. For myself, that meant no football, no BB gun, no motorcycle.

For my Dad, the issue was more nuanced. As a strong Nixon conservative Republican, Dad saw the world rapidly changing during his young adulthood. I believe this is partially why we moved in 1967 from Orlando, FL back to East Tennessee. The world was changing and the last thing my father wanted to see

©2010 Carl Creasman

was his son drifting towards some rebellious worldview associated with riding a motorcycle.

The funny thing was that even if I had gotten a motorcycle, the concept of me drifting towards some leather jacket-wearing thug was highly unlikely. If anyone represented me on *Happy Days,* it was Richie. In fact, I think they copied my life to make the show (or maybe I copied them). In any case, I was the "good boy" who obeyed the rules and whose worst transgression was either shooting off illegal bottle rockets or the occasional curse word. My "transgressions" didn't really even emerge in my vocabulary till high school where our homeroom was a minefield of put-downs and verbal attacks and one needed all the weapons at his disposal to make it through alive.

So, I was in no way "tough" or "rebellious." But I *wanted to be*. Or, at least, I wanted to be cool. By the time I started high school in 1978, I realized that I was not cool, and, though we didn't use the word, I was probably closer to a geek or a nerd than I wished to admit. I mean, I did well in school, went to church, never got into fights; we were even one of the first in our town, perhaps all of East Tennessee to own a computer. My father, an electrical engineer who had worked on early computers in the 1960s while working in the "space program" in Florida decided (correctly) that the personal computer would change the world, so he wanted his kids "in on the ground floor." He researched all of the options and in 1978 purchased an Apple computer, the Apple II. I programmed my own computer game and enjoyed historical recreation in board games made by the company Avalon Hill. But, I wanted to be cool, and maybe tough, like Fonzie. If I could just have a motorcycle, I reasoned, I would be.

For the next 30 years, I would often see a biker and wonder, but I knew it was not in the cards for me. That is, till I turned 40. A lot happens to you when you turn 40. I had read about it, and actually had been accused of being in "midlife crisis" in my 30s due to all of my mental anguish about life and sometimes psychosis about perceived injustices. Yet little prepared me for how I felt mentally in crossing that barrier in August of 2004.

Over the next year, I really did go through all the mental gymnastics about who I was, where I was going, what I had or had not accomplished and what the

©2010 Carl Creasman

horizon looked like. I realized that I had done much, just not the things I had assumed or hoped I would. I was happily married for 15 years and we had three healthy girls, who are my pride and joy. Yet, something seemed amiss. As I thought about it, one thing I realized was that I often still lived in a way that was too concerned with how other people perceived me. In other words, I seemed to often live as if I still needed to impress or please my parents and the other important adults in my life.

Now don't get me wrong, understanding that life is a symbiotic relationship with others is crucial to life success. You can't get far if you run over everyone or ignore the needs of others or treat people as if they are annoyances that you have to put up with. But, one can take it too far in trying to please others and, in the process, miss enjoying your own life. For me, at least, this was where I really found myself in those next months after I turned forty.

So, by the fall of 2005, I determined to do something about it. As I prayed about what would be healthy and useful, I returned in my mind to 30 years prior and one of my greatest regrets---that I never got a motorcycle. I determined then that I would set out to rectify that situation. The journey of the next months would be thrilling, as I had to figure out how to tell my wife, save enough money to buy a bike, find a safety course, and generally determine if I could, indeed, be cool enough to pull this off.

So often, as a speaker and mentor, I am asked about finding your dreams or how to accomplish a set of goals. When I was a professional swim coach, part of the job entailed helping others meet their personal athletic goals. Now, as a professor, helping others is a bit more tangential to the task of teaching history. Nonetheless, part of what I do is mentor students, teaching the skills necessary to reach their goals. For this task, I was going to need to put every bit of my learning into action to accomplish my dream of becoming like Fonzie.

©2010 Carl Creasman

CHAPTER 2

Make goals to achieve your dream: Planning the Ride

My purpose in writing this story is to make the concept of dreams and goals more real. Often it feels as if the information about actually going after a dream never connects. Thus, my hope is that my own story of fulfilling a life dream, using my own time-proven methods, strategies, and life philosophies, will inspire you to also take the necessary steps. Usually, we just sit around wondering, doing nothing, or only doing the same unsuccessful things as we've always done. That gets us nowhere different, of course, so if your dreams mean starting something new, well, just going the same way won't help.

We are awash in too many people with too small visions who never really get off pause in order to accomplish anything. Along the way, they find themselves in settings like I did, wondering if their life mattered at all. For me, the clear evidence is that I have already accomplished great things. Oh sure, I'll probably never end up in any history textbook, but I know how many lives I have impacted for the better. For all of my

©2010 Carl Creasman

adult life, I have helped shape the lives and beliefs of many. I have counseled people through the worst times, and in anticipation of the best times. I can't count the number of times people have said "you've changed my life for the better." And with those things, I am honored.

I actually think my problem comes not from having no goals or doing nothing, but from having visions that are massive! You may have heard of Jim Collins' concept of the "BHAG"—big hairy audacious goals. I think often that my dreams and goals are even bigger than that. Once, in a conversation with a friend, someone who is every bit as motivated and smart as I am, he countered one of my musings with "how do you really believe that you can change the world; I mean, that's pretty big for a dream isn't it?" I responded with "I can't help but try; to not fight for what I deem important—the future of my descendents and this country—is to live a small life."

So, perhaps my discontent in my 40s isn't the same as yours, or maybe you too wish to be a world-changer. Well, here you are. You are reading this book now. You have the same next minutes and hours as I do. What will you do with it? Where will you go? What can you change? What will you begin?

©2010 Carl Creasman

For my own journey, I am constantly in motion. My wife tells me I have no concept of how to rest and relax; she is probably right about that. Still, to not live every day to the fullest is a waste of our souls. By being constantly on the move, I know how to organize and prioritize and accomplish. With that knowledge and determination, I knew what I had to do to get my motorcycle. I had to start with a clear plan based on clearly defined goals. I wrote about goal-setting in my book, *Success for Life: Answers to the 77 Hardest Questions College Students Ask.*

One of the many jobs I have held was as a Swimming Coach for two different United States Swimming clubs. I have worked with Olympic athletes and former Olympic coaches. One summer I served as a visiting faculty member for Olympian Mary T. Meagher's swim camp.

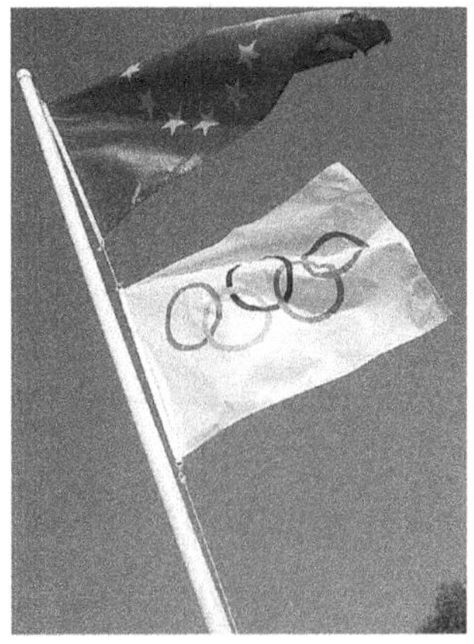

We constantly stressed and taught goal setting and I routinely incorporated the Olympic level of goal setting for my younger age group swimmers. You are never too young to set goals in life.

For our purposes, here are some key ideas that must be part of your plan.

- Goals must be something you write down.
- Goals must be something very specific.
- Goals should be in line with your deeper dream and purpose.
- Goals should be realistic based on your current situation, challenging but not impossible. This is where you may take a much longer goal (say a goal to be the CEO of a major corporation) and break it down into more realistic shorter-term goals (graduate in business, get hired by a Fortune 500 company, get MBA, get promoted to Management, and so forth till your ultimate goal of CEO).
- Goals should be track-able—these measurements are like mile-markers on the Interstate highway.
- Goals should be personal, something you have some degree of control over.

©2010 Carl Creasman

So, as I decided in the fall of 2005 to get a motorcycle, I knew I needed to establish clear goals. Now I already hear some of you laughing at me. You are thinking I could have just gone down to any bike shop, slapped down the credit card and been riding away in 24 hours. I suppose, but I didn't want to just own a bike; I wanted to live a successful life while enjoying my bike. That meant more than just tangibly having a bike in my possession.

For me, I knew that there were at least three major areas that had to be researched and planned in order to get to my dream. First, I knew that I'd need the money to buy the bike. My wife and I have lived our years of marriage with a clear principle of owing nothing on credit. While we've not always been perfect with this, and do use a credit card for many things, we have lived our married life this way quite happily. Sure, we haven't owned all the various things our peers do and we don't take as many trips as some around us. Our kids know that the majority of things they wish for at birthday time or Christmas are not coming. Yet, buying with cash and refusing to get into debt has worked for us, so I wasn't going to change that now to buy a motorcycle.

10 Carl Creasman www.CarlCreasman.com

To get to the right price, I also knew I needed a goal of finding out more information about motorcycles. That would involve some Internet work, but I like working with people and I already knew that I had a great resource at the College where I work. Gar Vance, the Assistant to the Provost on the East Campus of Valencia Community College when I was in this hunting process, has been riding motorcycles since the 1960s, so he would become my #1 resource in pricing bikes.

Another goal tied to price would be determining what kind of bike to ride. This one was easy since Fonzie was my inspiration. In the early episodes, Fonzie rode a Harley-Davidson; later the production team switched him to a Triumph. In either case, he rode a traditional "cruiser." Now, if you've looked around in the past 20 years, you know the more popular style of bike is the Japanese racing style, often called a "crotch rocket" for their speed and handling. Many of my friends have urged me to go this way, but with Fonzie as my mentor, there was no way I wouldn't get a cruiser.

©2010 Carl Creasman www.CarlCreasman.c

Once this was determined, Gar helped me see that I would need to find about $2000 to get a nice used, small motorcycle. I knew generally I could do that; now, with a clear, discernable goal, over the next months, every time I found any extra money, did overtime work, sold anything on eBay, that cash would be put into my "Bike Collection." Having done this previously for other purchases, most recently our one and only flat screen TV, I was confident.

Why "small" you ask? Well, I'll tell you more about this in a subsequent chapter but the basic goal here was knowing what I could afford and also knowing what my own safety level would be. As I said earlier, though I might wish to be cool and dangerous, I really wasn't. I have a very low threshold for taking risk, so knowing that, I knew there was no reason to start off on some larger bike.

That idea of risk led me to the last major goal—finding a good safety course. I know, you are laughing again, thinking is silly to find a safety course. Well, for me, safety needed to be front and center. My wife was very supportive of this dream for me, she couldn't wait to ride behind me (I think secretly she wants to drive

010 Carl Creasman

herself), but she also wanted me to be alive in the decades to come. Certainly we have no promises of life, and I would more likely be killed in a car accident than one on a motorcycle, but one doesn't need to "tempt fate" by doing something dangerous with no training.

Setting clear and consistent goals is a must if you really want to succeed at achieving your dream. You must not allow yourself to merely dream and then sit around hoping. I've read a lot, and seen others talk about, having positive mental energy in relationship to your dreams. While the merits of this "positive thinking" can be debated at some other time, I'll concede that keeping positive is important. However, in no way, and under no circumstances (that I have ever seen) does mere positive thinking replace taking concrete, goal-centered action.

©2010 Carl Creasman

CHAPTER 3

Know What the Dream Requires: You need the safety course

By early 2006, I was ready to begin. I was actually ready around the holidays, but knew that trying to start a safety course then was silly. Plus it might be cold. In the meanwhile, I recruited a friend. Going on your journey of *Success for Life* is so much more fun when you take a friend or partner. So, I asked my friend, Chris Delaney, to join me. My hope was that he would also get a bike so we could ride together.

First, though, I needed to find the right safety course. Now, again, you may be wondering why I needed that. Why not just go for it? Well, the answer starts with an ancient philosophy of "Know Thyself." Clearly, riding a motorcycle is dangerous, as is driving a car; however, riding a bike puts your physical body at greater risk than being in a car. One of the core concepts of being a good and safe rider starts with understanding your own threshold for risk.

The best illustration I can give for this is snow skiing. I have been skiing a handful of times and would consider myself a below-average recreational skier. In the times I have been skiing, I have ventured to look at the "Black Diamond" slopes. If you know about skiing, you know the Black Diamond is a universal symbol on ski slopes to indicate that the hill is for experts only. Now, to put it into perspective, most black diamonds seem simple for the Olympic level skier, but to a novice, well, it can look like a cliff.

For 3 years in the mid-90s, I was the college student minister to a church in Winter Park, FL. While there, I took the students skiing all three years. That first year was my only third time to ski ever, so I was very rusty. One of the lifts at the ski resort, Winterplace, in West Virginia, took skiers to a Blue slope (medium difficulty) as well as to a black diamond. I remember one day inching over to the edge of the black, looking as my skis carefully extended over the edge, and I promise you, the slope completely fell away at about a 45° angle. Perilously perched, I began to sweat and felt queasy in my stomach, thus I slowly began to inch away.

Two years later, after coming to the same place

©2010 Carl Creasman

both years, I attacked that same slope and made it down. I learned a valuable lesson on the way down, however. You can't ski down a Black diamond "carefully" or "slowly." On a "bunny slope" or even a "Blue," the beginning skier can inch their way. You can take wide sweeping turns, basically skiing sideways down the hill, and eventually get down the hill. Most Blue or Green (beginner) slopes are very wide, giving rookies like me space to mess up and still recover. The good skiers stay off those slopes just in order to NOT have to mess with people like me. Yet, you cannot go side to side on a black, at least not slowly.

You have to allow the skis to run and let the speed work. You are safer by accepting the risk. However, if you can't let go of the fear, then the best thing is to stay off the slopes. My point is that you can't ski scared. Know thyself. If your risk threshold is too low for a Black Diamond, then don't go on it; you'll probably get hurt!

The same truth applies for a motorcycle. You can't ride scared. You can't go so slowly to "avoid trouble" because you'll just end up BEING the trouble on the road. Think about the poor expert skiers risking their own lives trying to avoid you on the very narrow "black diamond" slopes. Well, expert car drivers will also have to weave and serve around you if you are riding slow because you are afraid or trying to "be safe."

Think about what happens to you when you end up "in over your head" If I had tried to actually ski that slope in my first trip to Winterplace, I doubt I would have made it. Even three years later, it was a tough experience. Imagine crashing on the hill and then trying to stand back up to start, all the while standing on a 45° slope and then turning to head down that same slope. In one crash I saw, one of the person's skis slid down the hill about 30 feet (that's a long way to crawl and still avoid getting hit by other skiers). Now, imagine the wreckage that occurs to the person who crashes their bike. Still think the safety course is a bad or silly idea?

But how can you or I discover your risk threshold with a bike? What if I thought I could do it, then spent several thousand dollars on a bike, only to discover that at age 42, I was too afraid. That would be a dumb and wasteful move that would only have me end up poorer and embarrassed. However, a safety course would allow me to test my own limits to see if I could even ride the bike safely, and I wouldn't have to purchase anything.

©2010 Carl Creasman

Many of the people that I mentor have very little understanding of their own limits, who they are, what they really want. Often, my first efforts with them are to have them try to get inside themselves; this can be a slow and painful process, but a necessary one. You see this a lot with students. They may know that they should come to College, but they often have no idea why. Sometimes, it is clear that they should NOT be in College, at least not yet.

But you can't convince them of that. So, they'll waste thousands of dollars for classes that someone said they had to have in order to get through some degree that someone else said would net them a lot of money in the future. What happens? Often, they hate every day and often drop half or more of their classes, wasting even more money and time. They won't really focus or learn in those classes in which they remain. Three or four years later, they'll wake up realizing that they've just thrown away some of the best years of their lives.

Or, I will often run into an adult who did complete College, did take the degree for the supposedly good job, only to discover that 10 years later, they hate themselves. Their job is a soul-sucking experience, or that their workmates are unpleasant. They'll drag themselves to work because they know they should, but deep inside they are dying. The problem isn't that job or that degree; the problem is that they have no idea who they really are!

I already knew I needed the course, but just in case I wasn't sure enough, God helped make up my mind through an incident with my friend Gar. He had spent the last 3 months helping me get ready and during spring semester, he rode to work one day. On our break, he put me on his bike. Now, Gar is a superior rider with hundreds of thousands of miles under his belt. He was riding a big Ducati at the time; I think it was a 1200cc, which is a very big bike.

Gar took the time to instruct me on the basics in an open area of our parking lot with no cars around. After a little jumpy start, I actually made a full circle. I was so pumped, but I should have sensed the problems.

©2010 Carl Creasman

To start with, I had no proper gear. I didn't even have a helmet on. The bike was clearly too big for me as a beginner, and worse, cars had begun to come into the lot where we were.

After enjoying my success, Gar told me to go again, but to change gears into second gear. You can see where this is going, can't you? Yep—after a successful start, I rounded the curve determined to shift to second, but I really had no good idea of how that happened. I knew I needed to do something with my feet, so I looked down, but then my throttle hand slipped and the bike revved. Remember, I'm on a very powerful Ducati and even though I was in first gear, it has power. So, as it lurched forward, I panicked when I looked up to notice I was going in a straight direction, towards a parked van.

Now, in retrospect, all I needed to do was grab the clutch and hit the brakes—no big deal. But, Gar had only barely told me anything about the clutch, which as any rider will tell you, is where all the magic and control is for any motorcycle. See, while my friend was a great mentor for starting to ride and finding the right bike, he was not going to be able to give me a proper safety course for the bike.

010 Carl Creasman

So, here's another key lesson to take away—you need the right kind of guidance. As you seek to "know thyself," certain desires and dreams will emerge. You will want to pursue them, but you'll need (or should want) guidance for the journey. Remember when I told you that I sought Gar out for his excellent advice? That was correct to do, but having him try to show me how to ride was not the correct thing. Maybe it could have been were we on the right machines, wearing the right gear, in the proper space, but we weren't.

With the van getting bigger in my view, I remembered where the brakes were and clamped down. Again, all the riders reading now know what happened. The bike seized up and slid sideways. Luckily for me, I was still going slowly enough (about 10 MPH) that I could control it as I got closer to the van, but I had no idea how heavy the bike was. Sure enough, as I tried to put my feet down, I realized this was not my bicycle from my childhood days where I could stop it with my feet. Quickly it pitched over about 1 foot from the van. Whew!!

I was okay. The van was okay. Gar's bike was only barely scratched, for which I felt terrible, but he quickly

©2010 Carl Creasman

claimed the accident was his fault (well, in one manner of looking at it, it was). The van driver was also a motorcycle rider and he felt bad for me, so he wasn't angry. My heart was pounding and I was shaking a bit. Only later did I realize that I had ruined my dress boots, ripping the heel off the shoe (I looked pretty funny trying to teach my next class 15 minutes later).

Lesson learned—off to the safety course. I did the research and found a very good, two-day course offered in Orlando. I rejected the quick-y course that places like the local Harley dealership did (2-4 hours). I wanted an immersive course and this certainly was, taking place for two 10-hour days.

We started in a class, going over a good safety manual and video series. Sure, I wanted to be riding like everyone else, but I knew the information would be critical. Then, after lunch, we hit the course. It was perfect; they started slow just showing us how to use the clutch (now I realized why I needed that info on Gar's bike). Before long, we were riding around and I knew--I could do this! You should have seen the smile on my face after we made our early passes around the track. When we took a break, I told my friend Chris that I was hooked and I would own a bike soon!

After the second day, we took our safety course test, which also served as the driver's license test. I passed with flying colors and I was on my way. Two days later, I was in line to get it added to my license and I was ready to take the next steps. I had invested in learning, not too proud to admit when I needed help. I studied my manual several times before taking the course (there were at least 3 people who failed the test). I paid attention to our teachers and made it through the road course well. I wasn't too proud to know my own limits.

©2010 Carl Creasman

CHAPTER 4

Earn the next step: Putting in the miles

Sometimes, we simply are afraid to face up to our own limitations. We think we are indestructible or that bad things will never happen to us. I am amazed when I hear these kinds of things from adults. Sure, working with children (under the age of 18) has conditioned my mind to accept that young people can't really believe bad things could come. For adults, one would hope that enough life had transpired to prepare them for the idea that challenges can come and that you must know your own limits.

I had already happily come to that conclusion while taking the safety course. We had some people in our course who actually had been riding previously, but they were just taking the course to get the license part taken care of. So, throughout the course, they really weren't paying attention nor thinking about their own limits. It is okay to have a higher risk level than others; I know that my risk threshold is low while one of my best friends, Matthew, has a very high-risk level. He'll try just about anything. Still, as these young men discovered by failing

)10 Carl Creasman

the course, acting carelessly about "this waste of time" simply undermines your own dreams.

Remember, this is the entire point of what we are trying to do—accomplish life dreams and experience *Success for Life.* While you are taking time to discover your own dream, you have to take into consideration what the limits are. Maybe to take the step you need, you must find $100,000 quickly. OK—are you really willing to deal with that amount of debt if you borrow it? Finding the money isn't as hard as you might think. You could apply for several credit cards all at once; even in our post-recession period of 2010, you can still find the applications for credit cards lying around. Or maybe you take out the second mortgage on your house. Or you convince your parents and a few other friends to take the risk with you. BUT, you must be willing to confront the limits.

Maybe what you are trying to do is become a writer. Are you prepared to put in the hours of writing knowing that most of your words will never be seen? Are you ready to write letters to the various publishing houses only to be rejected often? Does your risk threshold allow you to handle that much rejection?

©2010 Carl Creasman

In the same way that you need to think deeply through your dreams, you also need to consider your goals. Perhaps the dream is one that fits well within your life; my getting a motorcycle was in perfect alignment. Not only would it fulfill a life-dream and help me psychologically, it would allow me to save money on gas. This was the time frame when gas prices in America shot through the roof, so the notion of getting a vehicle that got 40-80 mpg was wise.

But I had to earn those goals. Buying my motorcycle was an example of that. If you know anything about bikes, you might know that over the years, they've gotten a lot bigger. When I was younger, you could often find someone riding a 75cc bike and then moving up to something bigger like a 125cc. A motorcycle is often described by the size of its motor and big road bikes that you might see on the highway have massive engines, often bigger than 2000cc. Anyway, back in the '70s, you could find a range going up from the 125—250, 500, 750 and then maybe over 1000cc.

Today, it's hard to find a smaller bike than a 500cc and often those are snorted at dismissively. Obviously, the bigger the engine, the heavier the bike and therein lies the problem for a starting rider. Most people can ride the bike easily enough once you are going, but as I detailed with Gar's bike, its in the stopping, standing, slow turning and other "non-rolling" moments that a heavier bike can cause issues.

Adding to that, the bigger motorcycles obviously go faster. While an expert rider wants to have the same power (and maybe more) than a car, that speed can get a novice into a lot of trouble. Motorcycles are easily the fastest "off the mark" so at a red light, a bike can quickly zoom ahead, yet with so many "red light runners," that advantage can become an issue.

Lastly, a bigger bike would cost me more. I still needed to finish raising the money. As I said, with Gar's help, I figured that $2000 should get everything I needed to start, and I was right. But that was aimed at looking for a small, starter bike—probably a 250cc. Going bigger was only going to set me back in time; it took me a solid year to save the money I needed and once I got the license, the last thing I wanted to do was sit around hoping to get a bike some day.

For me, this all clearly pointed to the idea of knowing my own limits and also of earning the next

©2010 Carl Creasman www.CarlCreasman.c

step. We've discussed the first point, so let me hone in on the second point. Often, as people are trying to reach their dreams, they fail to see that time will need to be employed. There will be steps to be accomplished and "stripes will need to be earned." You won't be able to just move into the CEO's office after a week on the job.

This is lost on many. After a few years of effort, some will simply crash and burn because they can't understand "why it's taking so long." You have to know that in life, success is never merely given, but always earned. Recently, a good friend of mine was hired as a national consultant. He had spent years as a wonderful Christian communicator, had helped hundreds of people through counseling and was seen as a mentor by many people, but he wanted to go further. When he first encountered this new company that works nationally with churches, he didn't just throw out his resume assuming he "was due." Instead, he "earned the right" to join the conversation by visiting this group in conferences, going to their training seminars and then doing work with the company regionally, almost all of it for free or for very little financial benefit. Then, as his status rose, the company noticed him and offered him

10 Carl Creasman

a great opportunity to work with them on a national platform. I am confident he will excel as he has earned the opportunity.

So, I planned to "earn the right" to ride a bigger bike. Gar helped me look and sure enough, after some scouring through the local bike sales ads, we found a couple of good options. Once I had the roughly $2000, I made a few phone calls and before long, I was driving in my pickup to get my new motorcycle.

After 30-plus years of wishing, I actually was going to own my own bike! I got a sweet Suzuki GZ-250 for less than $2000, which meant I had enough to get the gear I would need. I had saved the right amount and was able to pay in cash. My life dream of not being in debt was secure. The bike is a gorgeous "candy apple" red color with a neat little windshield. It only had a few thousand miles on it, so it was basically brand new.

I was so excited. Sure, some people gave me "grief" for having a smaller bike, but that was fine with me. I

©2010 Carl Creasman www.CarlCreasman.c

was going to be like "The Fonz." Still, I did not miss their objections either. A 250cc bike is slow and slow on two wheels means that you might have an issue getting out of trouble if a car wasn't paying attention and didn't see you. Or, riding with my wife, Kim is more of a challenge on my smaller bike. With the size of my bike, I certainly could not try to go on the Interstate without risking my life.

So, why didn't I just get the bigger bike? Many told me to, warned me that within 6 months I regret it; they were wrong. This is the main point—I needed to earn the right to be on a bigger bike. I knew that even though it was slow, that fact would protect me. I wouldn't find myself driving at a speed I couldn't control. The 250cc was only a bit bigger than the bikes we had trained on during the safety course. I was confident about my ability to handle that bike. I also needed to earn the money rather than stupidly getting into deep debt. Well, I did save up the money, so that part was covered, but earning my ability to ride? Not yet.

To get to that last point, "earning the ability to ride," I set another goal. I would spend the next 3-4 weeks riding often in my neighborhood and around my house to various errands before I started riding to work. Yes, I had been to the safety course. I had gotten the license. Yet, my experience was little more than 6-7 hours on the bike, and at the safety course, all we really did was go around in circles, never really getting above 15-20 mph. In other words, it would be a lie for me to act like I had the experience necessary to ride openly in the world.

Of course, to get the experience, you have to actually ride. It's a classic "Catch-22" situation. You don't have the hours on the bike to ride on the big roads, but you need to ride on the roads to get the time in on the bike. So, though it may have seemed silly, I really did ride only around my neighborhood. It was fun and it allowed me the chance to practice the various lessons from the course.

After several days of riding, I decided I could risk riding the motorcycle to run an errand to our Post Office. That building is located on a larger road, a big 6-lane "highway" road that I would also take towards my work. I can still remember my nervousness rolling up to the light that took me "out into the world." I knew, and reminded myself, that no one around me would know I was a new rider. There was no "driver in

©2010 Carl Creasman

training" sign I could hang on my back. I just had to put everything into practice—spacing, riding well, watching all cars around me, staying out of their blind spots, and effective starting and stopping.

I made it! I can still remember coming into the house and announcing to my wife, "I'm ready." The next morning I rode to work and it was great. My friend Gar had told me that every time he gets off his bike, he still has a big smile acknowledging how fun the ride was. I had that smile on my face. Now, it's been 3 years later, and I still smile broadly as I ride! Better, I know I can do it; I can ride safely. I have earned the right to my place on the highway, on my bike. I am already beginning the journey of again saving my money to get a bigger bike. I've earned the right to ride a faster bike. I have proven to myself (and my wife) that I will drive safely.

Don't be afraid to take your time in reaching your goals. It does little good to try and race ahead, getting into a position for which you aren't prepared and then suffer a major set-back that harms your overall life goals.

)10 Carl Creasman www.CarlCreasman.com

5

Prepare for negative outcomes: Are you wearing the safety gear

I can still remember the joy of looking at my sweet red Suzuki GZ-250 as it sat in my driveway. I even risked a short ride around the neighborhood the night I got the bike home. Thrilling. Sure, it was only a 250 and as I wrote above, it was small for me, but man, was I smiling when I got off. And then I parked it. That's right—I parked it in my garage and didn't ride it for about 2 weeks. That's right—before I did the training rides in the neighborhood, I had to let the bike sit unused.

What? I can hear your laughing at me right now, but I had a problem---I still needed to get all the right gear. I didn't have anything I really needed to ride the bike. Remember, I took the course where they provided everything. I just showed up and they gave us a bike to ride and a helmet to wear. I used old lifting gloves to ride and had my dress boots (yep, the same ones that I had ripped on Gar's bike). We only had to have on long sleeves because the training course keeps you at only about 15 MPH, so there's little danger of a big crash.

To start riding through the neighborhood or to

©2010 Carl Creasman

work, however, would have me out on major surface roads and I needed to dress properly for the experience. Of course, if you have been on the roads in some states, you might think something different. Here in Florida, it is true that many people will ride in nothing more than a T-shirt and shorts. However, what is true for others doesn't have to be true for you. This concept is also true in life. Yes, some will do what is unwise or dangerous or risky, and get away with it, but that does not mean you should go down that same road.

Before I would start riding, I knew that I needed to get a helmet. I also wanted a proper riding jacket and gloves, so I began the search. First I tried out some local places, but nothing seemed to fit right. In my desire to start riding, I could have just gotten something quickly, but the experts at the safety course had warned us about this. They said that you needed to put the helmet on for a while and wear it around the store to see if it started to hurt or gave you a headache. Worse for me, I had a large head, often wearing hats that are 7 3/4ths sized, but even helmets that size didn't fit well.

The stores I was looking in where your basic "big box" type motorcycle stores, so I did more research

10 Carl Creasman www.CarlCreasman.com

and discovered a place in Daytona Beach that only sold helmets. I loaded up the family and headed out. Sure enough, the experts at the specialty store helped me out; after trying one helmet the correct size, yet still uncomfortable, the expert suggested that perhaps my head shape was more oblong than round. He suggested a helmet by Arai, designed for my head-shape.

Success; by the end of the day, not only did we have a nice helmet for myself, but also helmets for my wife and daughters. Later, I purchased gloves and then completed the outfit with an official bike jacket that contains the lightweight "armor" to help in case of accidents.

Do you see the larger point here? The obvious point is simple; if you have a wreck on a motorcycle, your body is much more exposed. While in a vehicle, you really only need to worry about wearing your seatbelt because the car metal body and air bags will help protect you greatly. The only air bags on a motorcycle are when you fly off the bike and air billows through your shirt. Not really all that helpful. Yet, that is not the main point.

©2010 Carl Creasman www.CarlCreasman.c

In life, bad things will come your way. The negative result can happen regardless of your plans. This reality is missed by so many. I've read many journals and blog entries about finding success and they can often paint a "pie in the sky" picture. Just think happy thoughts, believe in yourself and 'poof,' you make it. Well, good things can certainly come, and believing in a hopeful future is wise, but it's not enough.

Proper planning is like playing the chessboard without moving the pieces. The further out you can visualize, the stronger you are! We know the chess masters can often see 5, 6 or even 7 moves ahead. The world expert Garry Kasparov was asked this question about seeing future moves. Kasparov replied that it depended on the positions of the pieces. "Normally, I would calculate three to five moves," he said. "You don't need more.... But I can go much deeper if it is required." The interviewer went on to share that Kasparov explained, "for example, in a position involving forced moves, it's possible to look ahead as many as 12 or 14 moves."

I was only an average chess player back in high school and I could only effectively see 3 moves ahead.

010 Carl Creasman

Often, I even missed some of those outcomes, but that is not surprising for a young chess player. Such is not surprising for a young person in life either. Skill in chess, as with skill in life, comes through experience; wisdom is built over a lifetime. Yet, the point remains that you must visualize all of the available moves . . .including the bad ones.

I was counseling a client once about a situation. As we talked, it became clear that he had not really postulated his response to the possible negative outcome, so I asked him about it. His response was staggering—"Ah, that won't happen."

While the boldness is commendable—we must approach our determined actions with boldness and, as Goethe stated, "boldness has genius, power and magic in it"—yet blindness to the coming blow is not boldness, but foolishness. Far too often I see this with my clients and friends. They make a decision; embark on some plan of action and never take the time to think about what will happen if the negative outcome comes.

Certainly we cannot know what will happen ahead of us. We make our best choices and do everything in

©2010 Carl Creasman www.CarlCreasman.co

our power to get to a positive result. Yet, things happen. Sometimes, as Jesus Christ stated, "rain falls on the just and the unjust," and that stinks if you happen to not have an umbrella.

You are certain the job will come through, but what if it doesn't? You are confident that the other person will come to you asking for forgiveness, but what if he doesn't? You know your spouse or partner will pay all the bills, but what if they forget? What if the bank doesn't make the payment on time? What if the car breaks down?

Every time I ride, I say a short prayer asking for protection and I leave my house prepared to ride carefully. I have no plans to crash, nor drive foolishly so as to lose control. Yet, each day, even when its 100° in the shade, I wear my helmet, gloves, long pants and jacket. As you approach the ride of your life, you'd do well also to wear the right gear and prepare for all possibilities and results.

Taking responsibility: Driving Defensively

In the safety course, our teachers, both of whom had been riding for 20+ years, stressed again and again that the majority of dangers for a biker comes from the others on the road. One study that I heard on the radio said that over 75% of all accidents involving a motorcycle come due to some negligence on the part of the other vehicle driver.

I know that some accidents for bikers come from their own stupidity. I've heard the same, sad accident reports as you have that state the injured (or dead) biker was going 120 mph on the highway, not wearing a helmet. But the evidence indicates that those people are the exception, not the rule.

I had heard this already from Gar who told me that both of his biker incidents (remember, he'd been riding for almost 40 years) came from a car driver who was not paying attention. In fact, Gar urged me to replace my bike horn with a truck-sounding horn.

The typical motorcycle horn sounds like something

©2010 Carl Creasman www.CarlCreasman.c

you'd hear from clowns at the circus. It's pretty tinny and small. Not Gar's horn. When he showed me the Ducati, he blasted the horn and sure enough, it sounded like an 18-wheeler horn. It sure would get someone's attention on the highway.

What's the lesson? Life, to be lived successfully, demands that you take responsibility for yourself and your actions. Working with students, I am so amazed at how many of them approach life with an assumption that things should be done for them. Not just 20-year-old students though but many others that I interact with have the same poor approach. Many people live their lives not taking responsibility for anything.

That is no way to success. As I tell my students, you have to "own your choices." You should never assume that anyone is really looking out for you. Few, if any, will risk their own situation to try and protect you from some bad decision. Think about how few of your friends will actually "get in your face" when they think you are making a bad decision. Why? They don't want to risk the relationship, perhaps, or maybe they just think its too much trouble to try and warn you. You have to own your choices and decisions. Living your life this way is empowering.

As I began to ride, I needed to prepare to ride defensively, but this was going to take some adjusting. I've been behind the wheel for almost 30 years, so I drive with a lot of assumptions. To start with, I know how good I am at driving (or at least assume I am good). I also know that I bring a lot of experience with situations to my driving. I've slid on ice, hit a cow, hit a deer, spun out on a dirt road, driven on dark, curvy, country roads and slid off a "recently rained on" damp road. Those experiences mean that while driving, I am comfortable with risks based on the fact that I believe I can handle any upcoming situations.

I don't usually drive at "10 and 2" on the steering wheel. I have driven long stretches with my knee. I don't text and drive, but I do occasionally talk on the phone. I can judge distances pretty well to slide into small slots between cars. I know my stopping distance for my truck and my van. And, I know what I can and cannot do when put into a crisis situation.

Driving defensively on my motorcycle was going

©2010 Carl Creasman

to take some getting used to. Fortunately, my risk threshold was low, as I said. The safety course had also given us several good tools to put into practice, such as keeping a clear timed count between the bike and any vehicles ahead.

Because of my respect for the bike and what could happen to me, I had to take responsibility for myself once I got on the road. I also knew that I needed to make sure that I wasn't a liability to others on the road. Remember my story about skiing the Black Diamond? If I started riding my motorcycle on the road with limited experience, not only would I become a danger to myself, I could endanger others.

So, I put a plan into place. I knew I needed to spend time riding through the neighborhood. Remember how I told you about "earning the right" to ride my bike? It may have seemed silly to you when you read it, but as a novice rider, I simply would not take the risk to get into a situation that I was not prepared for. No one else on the roads was going to somehow know that I was a rookie driver.

They would not be looking out for me "special," nor should I be expecting that from them.

I had to be responsible; no one else should be responsible for me. When I finally did start riding more often, I had to stay "fully engaged." I could not ride my motorcycle like I drive my truck. Instead, I constantly check to see that I am not in anyone's blind spot. While riding, I often count out the time distance between my motorcycle and the car ahead of me. I am more aware of traffic lights, cars turning and oncoming traffic.

As you approach each day of your life, with your many choices and decisions, are you "driving responsibly" or are you just assuming that "someone" will take care of it? As a student, are you fully engaged, doing the work as required and putting in the hours of work to do as well as you can? At work, are you sleepwalking through the day, or are you actively putting your best effort into the job?

Once upon a time, most people in this country understood that no one was going to just "hook them up." Yes, the community would be there if you got into a terrible jam; your church would rally to your side if something like a house fire took everything from you.

©2010 Carl Creasman www.CarlCreasman.c

But overall, if you didn't plant your crops, you'd die of hunger. If you didn't sew up the tatters in your clothes, you'd end up with nothing to wear. If you didn't chop the firewood, you'd be freezing in the winter.

If you really want to stand out in your workplace, be the person who operates with a "responsible" mindset. Trust me—your boss and colleagues will notice.

Overcoming Obstacles: Handling the ride when it rains

Have you ever had one of those moments when your perfect plan all seems to come together? Nice moment, huh? Well, have you had a time when it looked like the plans were all going to work out, but then something completely unforeseen happened? It's not as fun as the first result, is it?

You have planned. You have set goals. You have attempted to be in the right gear, have thought about all the possibilities that you can, and are prepared to take responsibility. And then, out of left field comes something that no one could have seen.

In the months after I got my bike, I rode as often as I could. I loved finding different roads to ride on. I would look for ways to get more "seat time" on my motorcycle and loved just zipping around on little errands. I really was happy when I went to fill up and it cost me about $7, compared to the $60 for my truck.

However, nothing really prepared me for what would happen the first time I was riding home from

©2010 Carl Creasman

school and it started to rain. Living in Florida, one thing we all know is that it rains often in the middle part of the year, say March-October. One moment the sun is shining and then, whoops, rain is falling. So, sure enough, one afternoon as I started to ride home, I looked up to see dark skies coming. Within a few minutes, drops of waters started to fall.

There was no way out of this. Ok, I guess I could have ridden to some shelter and sat there, wondering when it would all end, but that was pointless. I typically have a million things to do and sitting around waiting on the rain to stop wouldn't help me get my work completed.

So I rode on. . .and got wet. It wasn't too bad. I actually kind of liked it; cooled me off from the Florida heat. And, being a Florida rain, it was localized and ended quickly. By the time I got to my neighborhood, there wasn't any rain, though I was still pretty wet. No problem; dry out the gear and I'd be ready to ride again quickly. But that little rain did nothing to prepare me for what would happen a few months later.

At the time I was starting to ride, I was the lead singer in a local band called Anodyne. We were starting

©2010 Carl Creasman

to work on our second CD and were tracking the drums at a small local recording studio. On the last day, we needed to come in for a final listen to the drums and then we were all going to go over to our lead guitarist's apartment to begin the strategy of "what to do next." The process of actually making a CD is very intense, so we had several steps left to go and this meeting was important for us.

I can still remember pulling out of the studio in order to head over to Kyle's place. Since I didn't need my guitar for this meeting, I had taken the opportunity to ride my motorcycle. The morning ride over had been sweet. The sun was shining and the day portended a

©2010 Carl Creasman www.CarlCreasman.c

fun experience. Three hours later, as we pulled out, I couldn't help but notice that the sky was rapidly growing dark. I was following Kyle, who was in his car; I think he and the guys were wondering what I'd do if it rained.

It was summer, and in Florida, the summer rains can be harsh, much worse than what I had experienced in the spring. I knew it could be rough, but I really had no idea what I was in for while on my bike. After we went about a mile, the sky broke in a torrent. Now, having lived in Florida, I've seen heavy rains and knew how bad it could be; this was one of those explosive thunderstorms. Better, (or worse) the lightening was its usual active self.

Before long, I couldn't see anything well. Water was settling on the roads deeply which made traction challenging. Kyle's place was a good 15-minute ride from the studio, depending on the traffic lights, so we had a ways to go. At one point, I could tell Kyle was worried about me and wondering if I wanted to stop, but by this point I was completely soaked and waved him on. After a while, the whole thing became funny to me. Certainly it was dangerous and I'm sure I

010 Carl Creasman

looked like an idiot to everyone driving around us, but I couldn't change the situation. Finally, mercifully, we arrived at his place, with the rain still pouring down in torrents.

When we got to the door of his place, I was sopping wet, so he had to go in and get me 2 towels. I basically stripped in the hallway, but now what? Our plans for doing some more work were being challenged with this situation. I didn't have other clothes, obviously. Fortunately, Kyle had some shorts and I could throw my clothes into his dryer. Before long, we all had a good laugh at my expense and soon were all hard at work on our music, having a great time.

I can promise you that life is going to throw bad moments at you. The question at this point is not "are you ready" but will you go through with a positive attitude. I know earlier I told you about earning the right, setting the right goals, riding in the right gear and taking responsibility for your actions. However, some things simply can't be planned for.

OK, sure, I could purchase some rain gear. I probably would if I started touring, taking long rides of hundreds

©2010 Carl Creasman

of miles. For now though, it's easier to just check the weather forecast. But in general terms, even had I checked the weather or had rain gear, I would have gotten hammered that day. It was bright and sunny that morning. It was actually quite nice when I went home that evening. It just so happened that when I rode in the afternoon, the bottom fell out, an event that no one could have predicted.

The point is not that you should be "ready" for those things, as if you could predict the event would come. We covered that ground already. Here I am telling you that unpredictable things, often bad things, will happen to you and the choice is whether you'll ride smiling or not.

While I was riding, I realized that I could do nothing. I couldn't even really plan what to do once I got to Kyle's place. I just had to ride as safely as I could. Before long, the hilarity of the situation came to me. Now, trust me, it was dangerous. The other guys said that at certain points, they simply couldn't see me in all the rain and they were genuinely afraid for me. Yet I rode on. I had to.

10 Carl Creasman www.CarlCreasman.com

You will have to ride on also! Or, you can choose to quit, pout, or get angry. Quitting might have made some sense at the time, but again, I didn't know how long the rain would last. Actually it rained hard for about 45 minutes, time I knew we needed. Pouting or riding angry would have only compromised my ability to handle my bike.

As a professor, I have seen this reality many times. Students, like other adults, have a variety of situations that come out of nowhere. Sure, many times the "bad things" that students address are caused by their own negligence (remember, wear the right gear) or they fail to consider all the options (remember, take responsibility). Other times, though, events are happening that no one can foresee.

I have had students have to deal with death in their family. One student discovered that his wife was facing cancer. Other things aren't as drastic, but still impossible to foresee such as losing expected financial aid, or even that a teammate in a group project ended up in the hospital on the due date of the project.

These kinds of things can't be planned for.

©2010 Carl Creasman

Sometimes, you are just out on your motorcycle and the sky opens up and pours down rain. How will you handle it? Chuck Swindoll made the excellent and obvious point when he said, "I am convinced that life is ten percent what happens to me and ninety percent how I react to it. And so it is with you. We are in charge of our attitudes."

I know that not every situation is a laughing matter. Sometimes, the best response is to cry and lament. But, even as I cry, I go forward. I continue to persevere. I keep riding. Stopping on the side of the road to cry (or to laugh) simply won't help. So, keep smiling. Maybe, for many of these unforeseen moments, you can even laugh, and others might laugh with you.

Achieving Your Dream: Enjoying the road the journey

It has now been five years since I first decided to pursue and accomplish this goal. Silly as it might seem to some, or unimportant to others, it meant a lot to me. Hitting my forties really was a challenge for me. I knew that I needed to embrace what I have taught so many others---to really go for your dreams and never look back.

In some of my talks with students, I will come across someone who is seemingly taking a long time to finish school. They might be an older student or someone who had to overcome some challenges early on, thus they are in their first years of college much later than their peers. I've had some students say "all my friends now have jobs, so I must be a failure." In my encouragement to them, I remind them that the clock ticks for all of us and the only question is will we get going. Whether we like it or not, unless something really tragic happens, months or years will go by and you'll either have gone for your dreams or you'll still be standing on the sidelines wondering.

©2010 Carl Creasman

In this instance, I was facing the same question. I had faced it before. I had to decide to go back to get a second Master's degree. I had to decide to risk it all after finishing my seminary degree NOT go into church work and coach swimming instead. Four years later I had to risk leaving a promising career coaching to go BACK to work in the church. In 1998, I had to decide to roll the dice again and start my own speaking work. At each turn, I faced the same fears and concerns that I did this time.

Would I go for my dream as I understood it at the time, or would I stick to the sidelines doing nothing? Well, after reading this, you know that I have always gone for it. And, each time I have accomplished something of what I set out to do. I always face challenges, though, as the road of my life, the journey itself, comes with surprises, twists, turns and the occasional downpour. Yet, I would not change the trip even if I could go back in time.

I told you how my friend Gar describes riding, some 30 years later; each time he rides, a big smile crosses his face. He'll get off the bike at the end of a ride and just smile, thinking "what a great feeling." Now, 4 years after riding a lot, I know what he means. Even though my trip to work is only about 10-15 minutes, I get off my bike every time reveling at the joy of fulfilling my dream.

I doubt that I'm as cool as Fonzie, but boy do I feel good. I love being able to tell my students, "I ride a motorcycle." I love the "secret" wave that all bikers, at least bikers on cruisers, have with each other (sorry, can't tell you about it; it's our secret). I certainly love saving gas, and I love taking long corners leaning into the turn.

None of that would have happened without deciding to accomplish my dreams. So, now, what about you? Are you ready to ride?

©2010 Carl Creasman

About the Author

Carl Creasman has been speaking professionally for 23 years to a wide variety of audiences here in the United States and abroad in such diverse places as Haiti and England. Carl grew up in a small rural East Tennessee community with no traffic lights and only two stop signs. A swimmer in high school, he had a potential scholarship to Auburn University when adversity hit with a major career-ending injury. Undaunted, He confidently headed to Auburn anyway where he was an elite student leader.

Carl began speaking during college and continued to do so while earning two Master's Degrees, one a Master's of History and the other a Master's of Divinity. Throughout his adult life, Carl has combined his ability as a communicator with his love of working with people. He has worked in diverse arenas such as coaching an

Olympic training swim team, working construction for a custom homebuilder and ministering as the Student Pastor of a local church.

Currently Carl is a Professor of History at Valencia Community College, one of America's top community colleges. Consistently filling his classes, he is a popular professor known for his inspiring lectures, his concern for his students, and for his challenging style of teaching that demands students strive for excellence. His student reviews tell a consistent story as reflected by a common statement—"you are one of the best teachers I have ever had; thank you for changing my life."

Carl owns two businesses, fronts a local rock band, and serves as the Pastor of a local church. He has authored four books as well as contributed to two European history textbooks. With his band, Anodyne, Carl has recorded 6 CDs, with the latest just releasing in November, *The Comfort of Chaos*.

Carl is married to Kim and they have recently celebrated their 20th wedding anniversary.

©2010 Carl Creasman

They have three lovely daughters, Logan, Meryn and Brynn. Since 1993, they have lived in Winter Park, FL, moving from Wake Forest, NC where Carl completed his seminary degree.

As a Professor, Minister and Professional Speaker, Carl mixes history and spiritual depth with motivational, value-laden stories to drive home a passionate message that will leave your participants "inspired, encouraged and ready to charge forward into life."

To invite Carl Creasman to speak at your school, conference, or church, contact:

Carl E. Creasman, Jr.

P.O. Box 2031

Winter Park, FL 32790-2031

407.949.4171 or creasman@mac.com

www.carlcreasman.com

©2010 Carl Creasman

www.ingramcontent.com/pod-product-compliance
Lightning Source LLC
Chambersburg PA
CBHW071849020426
42331CB00007B/1924

* 9 7 8 0 9 8 1 4 6 3 8 1 0 *